Natural Disasters

Tsunamis

by Julie Murray

Dash!
LEVELED READERS
An Imprint of Abdo Zoom • abdobooks.com

Dash!
LEVELED READERS

Level 1 – Beginning
Short and simple sentences with familiar words or patterns for children who are beginning to understand how letters and sounds go together.

Level 2 – Emerging
Longer words and sentences with more complex language patterns for readers who are practicing common words and letter sounds.

Level 3 – Transitional
More developed language and vocabulary for readers who are becoming more independent.

THIS BOOK CONTAINS RECYCLED MATERIALS

abdobooks.com

Published by Abdo Zoom, a division of ABDO, PO Box 398166, Minneapolis, Minnesota 55439.

Printed in the United States of America, North Mankato, Minnesota.
052024
092024

Photo Credits: Getty Images, Shutterstock
Production Contributors: Kenny Abdo, Jennie Forsberg, Grace Hansen, John Hansen
Design Contributors: Candice Keimig, Neil Klinepier

Library of Congress Control Number: 2023948527

Publisher's Cataloging in Publication Data

Names: Murray, Julie, author.
Title: Tsunamis / by Julie Murray
Description: Minneapolis, Minnesota : Abdo Zoom, 2025 | Series: Natural disasters | Includes online resources and index.
Identifiers: ISBN 9781098285524 (lib. bdg.) | ISBN 9781098286224 (ebook) | ISBN 9781098286576 (Read-to-me eBook)
Subjects: LCSH: Natural disasters--Juvenile literature. | Tsunamis--Juvenile literature. | Tidal waves--Juvenile literature. | Severe storms--Juvenile literature.
Classification: DDC 904.5--dc23

Table of Contents

Tsunamis

Tsunamis are giant waves of water. These powerful waves can wash over coastal areas and cause great destruction. They are **unpredictable** natural disasters.

Causes

Tsunamis are caused by **violent** movement on or near the ocean floor. This is usually from an earthquake. Underwater landslides and volcanoes can also **trigger** tsunamis.

TSUNAMI HAZARD
ZONE
IN CASE OF EARTHQUAKE, GO
TO HIGH GROUND OR INLAND

The movement pushes ocean water upward. This sends long waves out in all directions. Far out in the ocean the waves are small and flat.

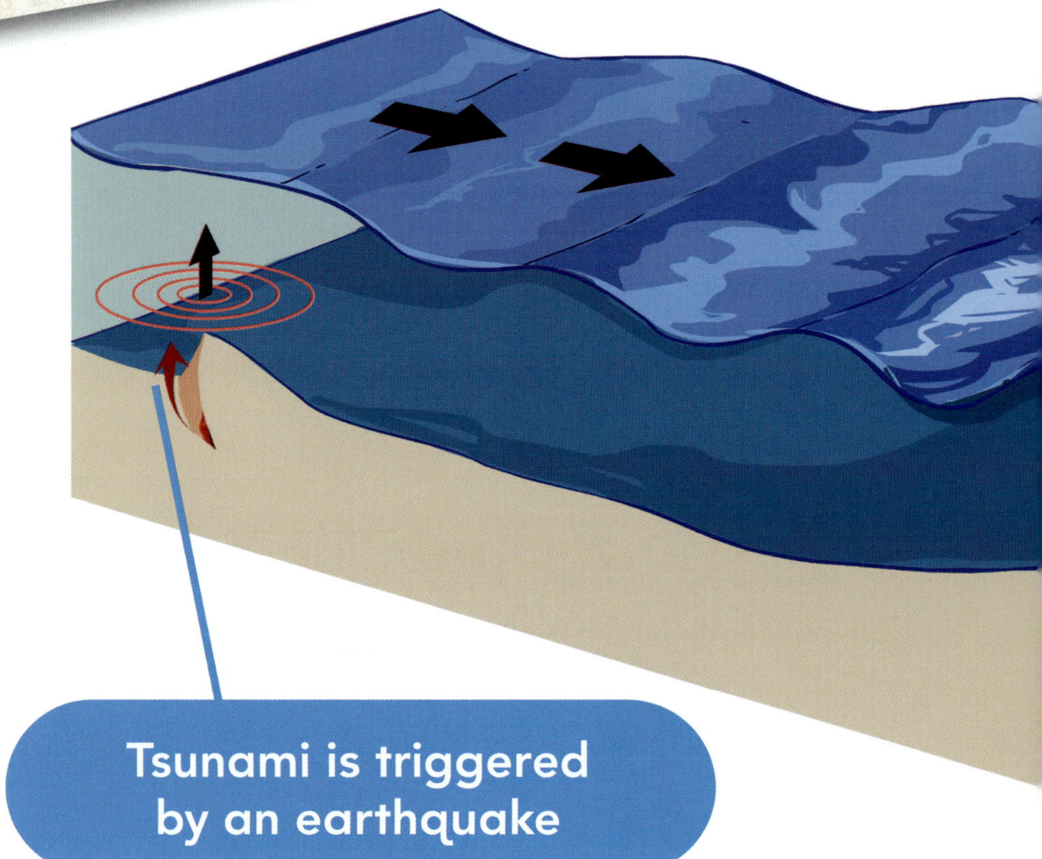

They can travel up to 500 miles per hour (805 kph)!

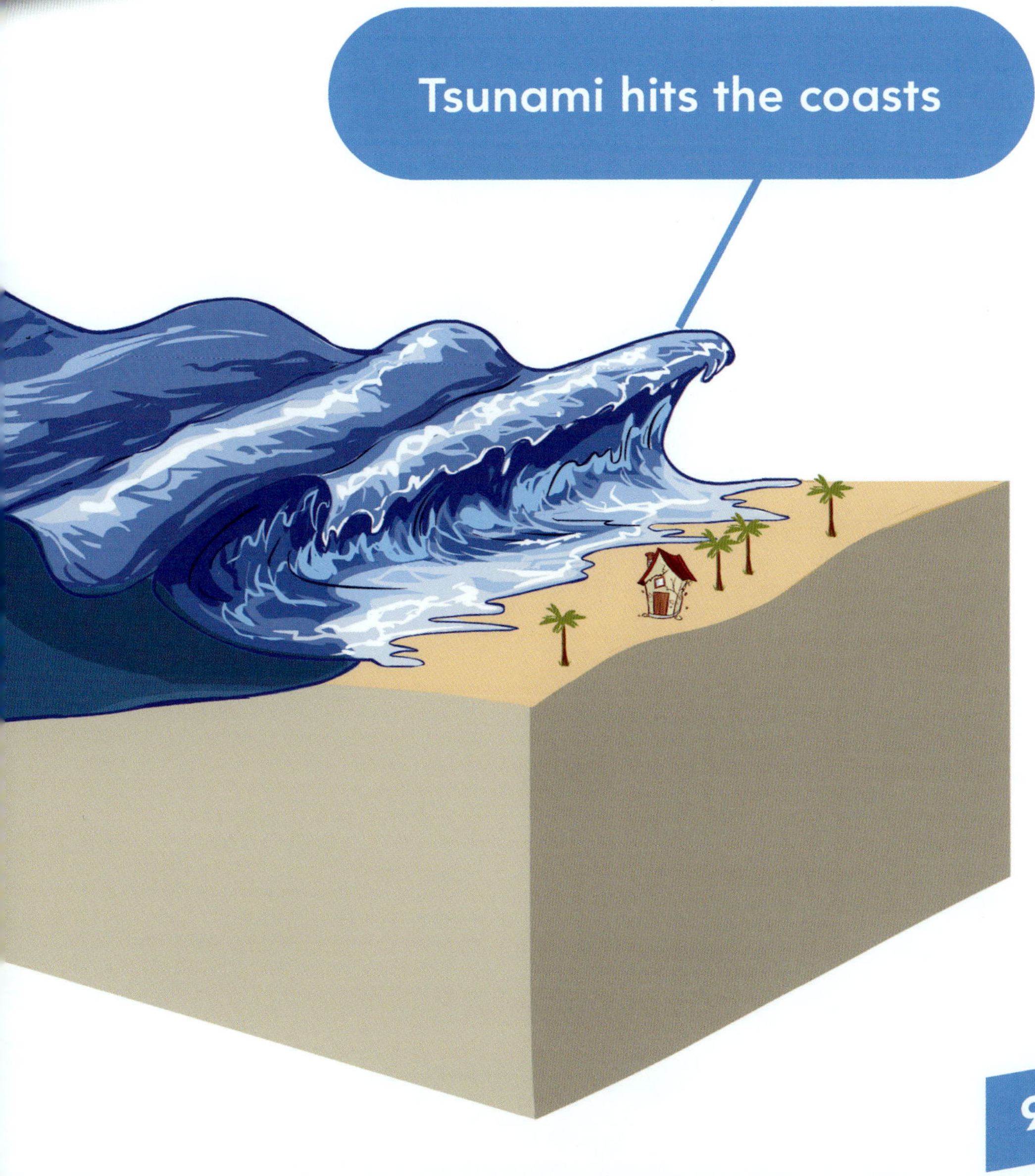

As the waves approach the coast, they drag along the ocean floor. The shallow water slows the waves down and builds them up. They grow to be walls of water.

12

Once the waves hit the shore, the water moves inland. The waves are so powerful they can destroy everything in their paths. Tsunami waves can last for minutes or hours. The waves can be close together or hundreds of miles apart.

Most tsunamis happen within the Ring of Fire. This is an area around the Pacific Ocean.

Most earthquakes and volcanic eruptions take place in this area. Tsunamis can also occur in other parts of the ocean and large bodies of water.

Effects

Tsunamis can sweep away people, cars, trees, and buildings. The water can travel inland up to 10 miles (16.1 km). The waves and flooding can be so powerful that they reshape the coastal landscape.

One of the deadliest tsunamis in history occurred on December 26, 2004. A 9.3 earthquake struck in the Indian Ocean. The tsunami that followed hit 18 countries. More than 230,000 people were killed.

Tsunami warning systems can track incoming waves. They can detect earthquakes and **monitor** waves moving across the ocean. This can give people time to get to higher ground. The warnings save people's lives!

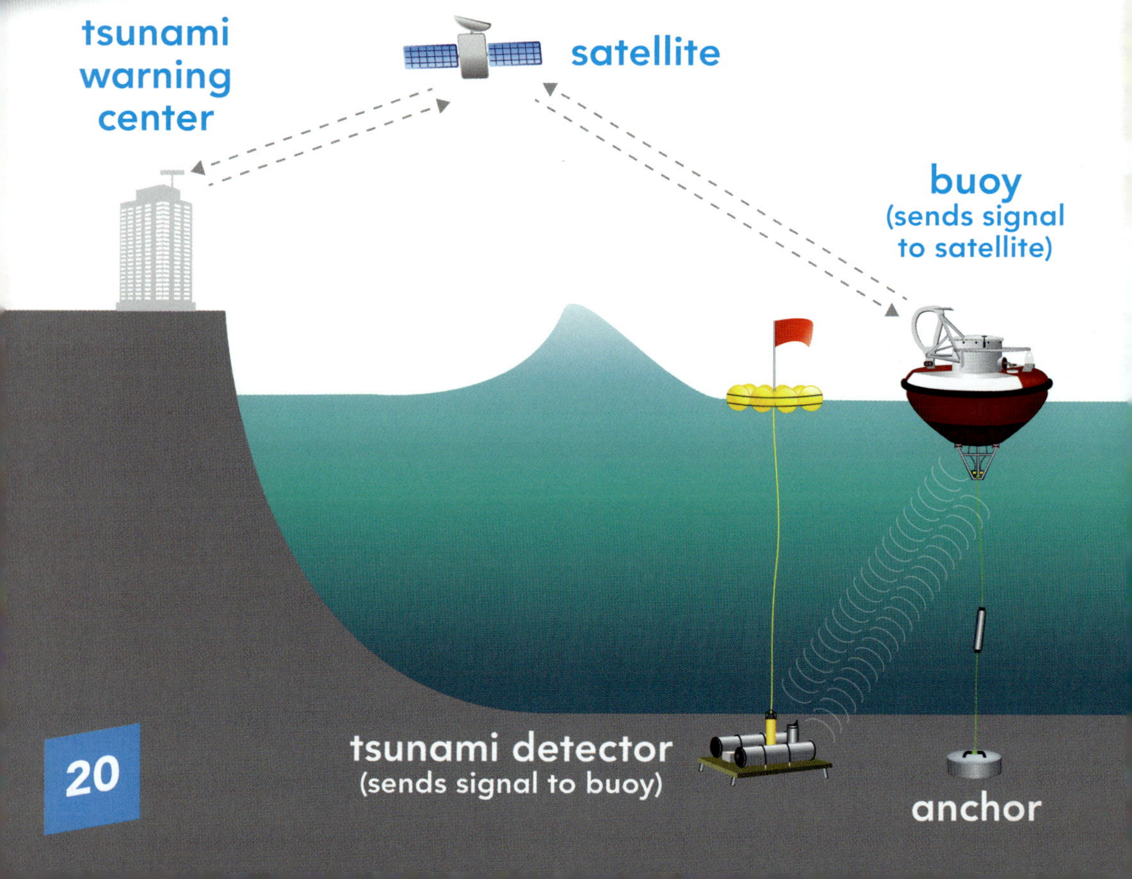

BUOY
TSUNAMI
RISTEK

More Facts

- Most tsunami waves are less than 10 feet (3.05 m) high. Some can be 100 to 200 feet (30 to 61 m) tall!
- The largest tsunami wave ever recorded hit Alaska in 1958. The wave was 1,720 feet (524 m) high! It was called a "mega tsunami."
- Japan is the country most affected by tsunamis. Hawaii is the most affected area in the US.

Glossary

monitor – to observe in order to check on.

trigger – to cause, begin, or set off.

unpredictable – not able to be known beforehand.

violent – very strong or harsh.

Index

Online Resources

To learn more about Tsunamis, please visit **abdobooklinks.com** or scan this QR code. These links are routinely monitored and updated to provide the most current information available.